THE ᴄ____._ ._. ...
GREAT PLAINS STUDIES
® *College of Arts and Sciences*

The Center for Great Plains Studies is a regional research and teaching program established in 1976 at the University of Nebraska. The mission of the Center is to foster study of the people and the environment of Great Plains.

A sparsely-populated region with highly variable weather set against grassy, rolling land, the Great Plains stretches westward from the Missouri River at Omaha and Kansas City to the Rocky Mountains, and northward from the Texas Panhandle into the Canadian Prairie Provinces.

The region invites inquiry into the relationships between its natural environment and the cultures brought to it by its various inhabitants, as scholars and residents work both to preserve healthy ecosystems and build thriving human communities.

The Center operates the Great Plains Art Museum, the Plains Humanities Alliance, undergraduate and graduate programs, various scholarly projects, and outreach programs; it publishes Great Plains Quarterly and Great Plains Research; it presents public lectures and interdisciplinary symposia. Much of its work is accomplished by its Fellows and Associate Fellows.

Nebraska
UNIVERSITY OF
Lincoln®

Created by the Great Plains Ecotourism Coalition

Written by

Rick Edwards
Director,
Center for Great
Plains Studies

Kat Shiffler
Ecotourism
Consultant,
Associate Producer,
Platte Basin
Timelapse

Katie Nieland
(design)
Communications
Coordinator,
Center for Great
Plains Studies

THE CENTER FOR
GREAT PLAINS STUDIES
® *College of Arts and Sciences*

TIME FOR ADVENTURE

Welcome to the Great Plains! This vast region, stretching from Texas to Manitoba and the Rocky Mountains to the Missouri River, contains many delightful things to see and experience. In this guide, you'll find just a few of the many places you can visit to encounter the region's immense grasslands, abundant wildlife, and enormous diversity.

Some people are fortunate enough to see wild elephants in Botswana's Delta or jaguars in Venezuela's Llanos, but it turns out Americans have similar treasures right here. Often disparaged as "fly-over" country or the "Big Empty," the Great Plains is, in fact, filled with biodiversity, critical habitats, and wonderful opportunities for you to have fun while deeply engaging with nature. You just have to find it. That's why we've made this Guide, and we've started by describing eight great places in Nebraska.

People travel for many reasons – for business, to visit family, search out new job opportunities, simple amusement, or to explore exotic places or cultures. Even before the founding of national parks, people traveled to remote sites to immerse themselves in nature, to breathe, observe, smell, and experience the out-of-doors. Today, many of us lead most of our lives in-doors, yet somewhere deep in our psyches we know that being outside in the open air brings many benefits – physical, mental, and spiritual.

That's why we send our children out to play, because "it's good for them." And it's good for us, too. But even for today's children, opportunities to be outside are severely limited, as the book *Last Child in the Woods* so powerfully documented. And when we do get out-of-doors, we tend to use our great open areas as a kind of natural playground for skiing, hiking, camping, hunting, fishing, and other recreational activities. Pleasurable as these activities are, they are in essence one-sided: we draw on nature for our benefit.

But as concern for the health of our planet increases, people want their travel to have more meaning. That has spawned a different and fast-growing form of travel with a different flavor – *ecotourism*. This is travel designed to engage with the environment and contribute to its survival.

Admittedly, much of ecotourism's fun is simply the joy of seeing: a wild elephant viewed from thirty feet away is an awesome sight, as is the endless to-ing and fro-ing, whistles, alarms, and frenetic activity of a prairie dog town. How many times have I seen delight and wonder on someone's face as she exclaimed, "I never knew ..." or he said, "I had no idea ..." upon first seeing a long-billed curlew. Jane Goodall, in Nebraska for the fifth time to view a half-million or more sandhill cranes temporarily gathered along a short stretch of the Platte River, labeled their migration "one of the seven wonders of the natural world." The Great Plains offers an astonishing variety of nature to absorb, experience, and enjoy.

But ecotourism invites us to do more: it puts us in an intimate encounter with nature, encouraging us to learn about the environment and how we can act to preserve it. Ecotourism stimulates our curiosity about the natural world, it builds our understanding of natural processes, and it helps us develop an appreciation of ourselves as nature's stewards. Ecotourism is today's version of following John Muir into the High Sierra or John Wesley Powell down the Colorado River or seeing Aldo Leopold's ethics of conservation and sustainability being put to work in specific locales and species.

Unlike Muir, Powell, and Leopold, most of us come from walks of life where we cannot devote our entire lives to nature. But ecotourism offers a way into their world. More importantly, it offers we who are concerned about the planet's health a way to combine enjoyable pastimes with something more meaningful and useful. Most vacation travel offers amusement and entertainment but little lingering effect. Ecotourism is different. It tends to transform one's consciousness in ways that affect us long after the trip is over, and it also helps sustain the enterprises and organizations who are stewards of natural places.

How ecotourism promotes conservation is simple but sometimes missed. If ranchers and other landowners want to attract ecotourists, they must provide protected habitat and sufficient wildlife to create a meaningful environmental experience. Ecotourists arrive and spend money for access, lodging, food, guides, tours, and other services offered by landowners and others in the nearby communities. And the cycle is completed when ranchers and landowners see they have an economic incentive and reap an economic reward for maintaining habitat and protecting the wildlife that attracted the ecotourists.

This Guide shows you eight of the many terrific opportunities here in the Great Plains where you can intimately experience nature. These privately-owned enterprises offer their visitors an environmental experience, a chance to see the region's natural splendors up close. But private enterprises aren't the only ecotourism providers – there are also sites run by non-profit organizations, national and state parks, and many other wildlife refuges and conservation areas. These different pieces work together, because successful ecotourism requires many kinds of services and providers.

These eight places are special. All are run by individuals and families, typically on the family's own land, and their cultural ties, working relationships, commitment to the environment, and knowledge of their surroundings make them unique. Their special character suggests they might serve as models for other private landowners. Most of the Great Plains – and 93 percent of Nebraska – is privately owned, so individual landowners play a huge role in the conservation of biodiversity.

To our knowledge, no other guide to these private ecotourism opportunities has been published before. We believe these entrepreneurs' efforts can add up to a mosaic of successful conservation. Ecotourism is a way to highlight them, gain public support, and celebrate them.

3

The Great Plains Ecotourism Coalition, publisher of this Guide, is a group of organizations and businesses committed to supporting and extending the infant but emerging ecotourism industry of the region. It is dedicated to promoting environmental conservation and building thriving human communities through nature-based tourism in the Great Plains. The Coalition includes both non-profit and for-profit members. An essay at the end of this book explores how ecotourism creates incentives for habitat and wildlife conservation, supports nearby human communities to be vital, thriving places, and generates additional revenues for ranchers and other habitat landowners.

For further information, see www.visittheprairie.com or www. go.unl.edu/ecotourism.

So go outside. Explore. Experience. And help ensure that there are natural areas to enjoy for years to come.

CALAMUS OUTFITTERS

SARAH SORTUM
Switzer Ranch and Nature Reserve
83720 Valleyview Ave
Burwell, NE 68823

http://www.calamusoutfitters.com
http://www.nebraskaprairiechickens.com
308-346-4697

Activities: Lodging, river trips, bird watching, jeep tours, ranch tours, specialty events, business/group retreats, hunting

Customer Base: Hunters and bird watchers from out of state (spring/fall), summer crowd is almost all in-state; mostly families

Facilities/Capacity: Two large-capacity lodges with a capacity of 20 people each; 4 rustic cabins along with modern amenities, each with 2-6 person capacity

Rates: Lodges on Friday and Saturday nights for $450/night, two night minimum; Sunday-Thursday for $400. Cabins are $75 per night double occupancy and $100 per night up to six occupants.

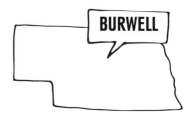

Wildlife at the Calamus River.

THE STORY

Located near Burwell in the north central Nebraska Sandhills, Calamus Outfitters is a family-owned business providing outdoor recreational activities for diverse kinds of tourists: hunters, serious birdwatchers, and families who want to float down the river or lounge at the nearby Calamus Reservoir, a prominent regional tourist attraction. Calamus Outfitters is based at the Switzer Ranch, a fourth-generation cattle operation. Bruce and his wife Sue Ann run Calamus Outfitters with their grown children Adam Switzer and Sarah Sortum.

The business started when Adam wanted to create additional income on the ranch by establishing a hunting lodge and guide service. The Switzers then began taking tourists on trips down the Calamus River that runs through their ranch. Eventually, Sarah came back to the ranch with her young family. To create yet another livelihood, she developed what is now the thriving ecotourism portion of the business: bird and wildlife viewing and interpretive jeep tours. Now an established birding destination, visitors flock to the ranch in the early spring months to witness the famously-odd mating ritual of the greater prairie chicken.

7

What you forget is that what we have here is different from what most people have. Most people live in town, and they don't have the chance to go out everyday and see this stuff. —Sara Sortum

The Switzers' version of ecotourism is regarded as a success story in Nebraska. But it wasn't always clear to the family that they had anything to offer the public. This changed when, early in the development stages, Sarah and her father traveled to Namibia with the World Wildlife Fund to observe wildlife safaris and ecotourism on the African continent. She describes a turning point on that trip, a day where they didn't end up seeing lions or elephants, but instead observed the subtle, yet equally special aspects of the wide open African savannahs on a guided jeep tour. She described it as the best day of all.

Sarah does an excellent job of sharing the raw beauty of the Sandhills, using stories to weave together information about what guests see. She points out medicinal plants of the Pawnee, checks in on the beaver that lives on Gracie Creek, and talks about their ranch management practices. "I always talk about plants, because you're not guaranteed you'll see wildlife, but those plants are always there. They're my bread and butter," she said. On the Sundowner Tour, she takes guests out in the evening, and in addition to stories, offers them wine and appetizers along with a stunning vista.

I like putting stories together. It's not just identification. It's 'what is the story behind it?'.

In fewer than ten years, the Switzers have created a reputation for themselves as the go-to place to get up close and personal with the Sandhills—especially its native grassland birds. In 2012, Sarah organized the first Nebraska Prairie Chicken Festival, an annual early-springtime celebration spread over two and a half days that is timed to correspond with the odd mating ritual of this threatened grouse species. People from around the country come to enjoy bird tours, speakers, and other activities.

Of all the activities they offer, Sarah says ecotourism provides an estimated fifteen to twenty percent of Calamus Outfitter's total **8** income—and this number grows each year. The majority of this income is accrued over the month-long prairie chicken mating season. During this peak birding season, Sarah and the Switzers transport crowds to observe the birds at dawn from a comfortable blind situated at one of the many booming grounds (where the male prairie chickens perform their mating dance) on the ranch. The mating dance of the sharp-tailed grouse offers another popular sight in early spring. Now that the word is out about Calamus Outfitters, Sarah and her family stay busy guiding birders. "It's definitely worth it. It's crazy for a while, but it's worth it," she said.

Sarah does not categorize their hunting or river trips—other major Calamus Outfitter's activities—as ecotourism. Instead, she distinguishes in terms of interpretation or education and believes that the summer-time river crowds aren't necessarily there to be immersed in nature. "It's still nature-based. People certainly enjoy it. They say it's beautiful. But that's not the key reason why they're going," she said.

"You have contact with the public and you have an opportunity there to spread awareness and to educate."

Sarah and her family walk the walk when it comes to conservation.

A greater prairie chicken. Photo: David R. Neilson

In 2013, the Switzer Ranch was once again recognized, along with their neighbors, with the prestigious National Cattlemen's Beef Association's Environmental Stewardship Award for their landscape-scale approach to biodiversity conservation. The ranch itself was designated an Important Bird Area by Audubon Nebraska in 2010. An international network of places recognized for their outstanding value to bird conservation, the Great Gracie Creek Landscape (the Switzers and two neighboring ranches) was the first privately owned site in the state to receive this distinction.

At the Switzer ranch, the family's Sandhills heritage runs deep. One of their biggest strengths is the family's desire to work and be together. They have the drive to make that happen, even through untraditional means.

"We want our family to be here in fifty years, in 100 years. Not only do we want our ranch to be here, our family to be here, we want the Sandhills to be here and everything we enjoy about it. We want the prairie chickens to be here and everything else."

Their personalities also seem to be a match for the ecotourism field. Sarah has the outgoing nature necessary for a tour guide. Her father, Bruce, is an old-fashioned, horse-riding cowboy character who is exactly who you'd want to meet around a campfire on a brisk, Sandhills evening. When one spends time with the Switzers, it's apparent their strong work ethic is the glue that holds the whole operation together.

In addition, the Switzers have forged important relationships with conservation organizations and university researchers. They collaborate often with the World Wildlife Foundation (WWF), The Nature Conservancy (TNC), Audubon, and the University of Nebraska, among others, and are able to call upon experts at these institutions for help with questions or special projects. Through these connections, they've been able to tap into the crowd of crane tourists that flock to the Platte River—a huge boon for their business. In 2013, the number of birders who visited the

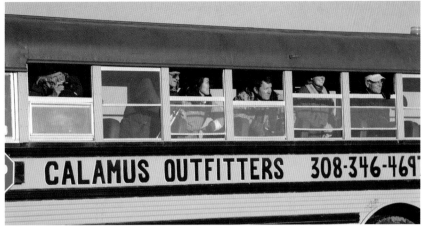

Sarah Sortum gives a guided tour at her family's ranch. Right: A jeep tour at dusk.
Photos: Sarah Sortum

ranch doubled.

The Switzers' innovative efforts and their abilities as communicators and networkers have led to media coverage in outlets including *Audubon Magazine*, Nebraska Public Television, and *The Washington Post*. Sarah has also secured grant funding for various projects, including a multi-state radio advertising campaign and a multi-year Nebraska Environmental Trust Grant focused on the conservation of threatened species on ranch lands.

> 99
> We've met so many great people through it. I think we've become better land managers because of [ecotourism]. It's made us aware of a lot of bigger picture things, like we weren't aware of the plight of grassland birds, and now it's a main focus of ours. So it's been an enriching experience.
> 66

Ecotourism and tourism in general have worked for her family as a diversification strategy. Through these additional activities, younger generations have been able to move back to the ranch and make a living separate from, but related to, their family's ranching business. "We're meeting our goals. We're all able to live here. We're able to raise our kids here," Sarah said.

NIOBRARA RIVER RETREATS

STEVE HANSEN
Schlagel Creek Ranch
PO Box 414
Valentine, NE 69201

www.niobrararetreats.com
www.schlagelcreekranch.com
402-322-0640

Activities: Lodging and camping, tubing, canoeing, guided nature walks, orienteering, catch and release fishing, nature photography, bird watching, overnight stabling and horseback opportunities

Customer base: Weekend tourists to the Niobrara; specializes in family reunions, multi-family gatherings, wrestling camps, church groups, and special events

Facilities/Capacity: Large, shared sleeping arrangement; can accommodate between 10 and 64 guests with seven bedrooms. Fully-furnished kitchen, large grill, big common dining hall

Rates: $25 per person per night, 10 person minimum or $27.50 for less than ten people. Multiple meal plans possible.

The sun setting on the road to the ranch. Photo: Steve Hansen

THE STORY

> We get people coming to the area because of the draw of the river… I provide the services for them, I do the tubing, canoeing and lodging, but I also try and expose them to the uniqueness of the river valley. —Steve Hansen

Steve and Debbie Hansen bought Schlagel Creek Ranch in 1985. At the time, Steve was working as a fisheries wildlife biologist in Alaska. "We bought the ranch because of the biodiversity here," he said. In his search for land, he took a scientific approach. Looking widely in the western United States, Steve overlaid data from state and federal agencies about various wildlife populations—deer, antelope, upland species, game birds, grouse, prairie chickens, turkey, fisheries, migratory waterfowl—and created his own maps. Steve recalled, "Any place that overlapped, I said in my mind 'that's a hot zone' because it's got all that biodiversity in one area." That's how the Niobrara River Valley caught his attention, an area where six distinct eco-zones come together, and where the Hansens now **14** call home.

In 1999, Steve and his family moved from Alaska to the Schlagel Creek Ranch located just five miles south of Valentine. They named their business Niobrara Riverview Retreats, an appropriate description of how they transform their love for the outdoors into a moving experience to share with visitors. On the website, they say:

"The vast unspoiled landscapes, abundant wildlife, its many area fishing lakes and friendly people (although we don't have many people out here... and that was part of the attraction, too) all convinced us that this is a pretty special place! We are now very pleased to be able to share the area's many bounties with you."

Schlagel Creek Ranch borders two miles of the Niobrara River and includes hiking trails and a 25-acre marsh appropriate for canoeing and catch-and-release fishing. This working cattle ranch has accommodations for a large number of visitors. The land features many things to see, including a wetlands restoration project and a marshland, and is surrounded by things to do in the Niobrara River Valley. The portion of the Niobrara designated a "Wild and Scenic River" is only three and a half miles east.

The Valentine National Wildlife Refuge is only fifteen miles away, a stunning landscape of more than thirty Sandhills lakes spread out across 70,000+ acres with 260 identified bird species. At nearby Ft. Niobrara **15**

National Wildlife Refuge, visitors can see bison, prairie dogs, elk, burrowing owls, and many other species. Both areas are internationally designated Important Birding Areas, two of only twenty such sites identified in the state of Nebraska.

The bird diversity here strengthens the attractiveness of Steve's operation as an ecotourism site. He even had a one-time sighting of a large group of endangered whooping cranes that stopped overnight on their migration north. Although the whooping cranes are an exception, spending time in the area is certainly an opportunity for birders to cross many species off their "life list."

Close by is the Merritt Reservoir, home of the Nebraska Star Party, and only two miles away is the Cowboy Trail, soon to be the longest continuous rails to trails project in the country. Such a trail is the conversion of a disused railway into a multi-use path, typically used for cycling and walking, and, in some cases, horse riding. Upon completion, the Cowboy Trail will extend 321 miles along the historic Chicago and Northwestern Railroad, from Norfolk to Chadron. Currently the trail's westernmost point is Valentine.

Steve decided to go into tourism because they couldn't make a living from ranching alone (he and his family do not currently own cattle but instead rent out their land for grazing). In addition, Steve's civil servant background prepared him to be an intermediary between the country's natural resources and the general public. The bottom line is that he likes showing and teaching people about the natural world.

> Because most of the stuff we do is non-consumptive, people come, they look, they leave. They just leave tracks. It seemed like a natural thing for us. We enjoy working with the public, and we enjoy sharing.

A Bronze Copper butterfly (Lycaena hyllus). Photo: Steve Hansen

Steve and his son share a background in collegiate wrestling, and conduct several week-long wrestling camps and college team-building retreats at the ranch each summer. Through wrestling and other word-of-mouth connections, they've also attracted big church groups for weekends.

Hunting is not the focus of Steve's ecotourism enterprise. Although he does have a background as a big game hunting guide, he currently limits the amount of hunting on his property. He called himself "stingy" when it comes to "selling off" the surrounding wildlife and also remarked that hunting hasn't been an economic focus for him compared to other non-consumptive activities, such as hosting events or river excursions.

Steve also created a geocaching course on his land. Geocaching is a popular outdoor activity where participants use a GPS or some other means to find hidden containers called geocaches. Steve sets up a competitive freestyle orienteering course for wrestlers and teaches them how to use topographic maps and a compass. He made a scaled-down version for guests where people find twelve stations using a GPS unit. He located the geocaches near plants of particular interest or next to geological formations or other natural features and also placed informational placards at each spot. Visitors can opt to take a self-guided, but interpretive nature tour and learn about the Ogallala aquifer. For example, they can pause **17** at the point where a layer of bedrock emerges and exposes an artesian well.

"I basically do all this so they can get a feel for the uniqueness of the ecosystems here along the river by just taking a hand-held GPS and going on a hike."

Steve is an expert naturalist who can explain his surroundings in detail. He speaks about botany, geology, biology, and ecology in relatable terms connected to his surroundings. For example, he can explain how, when floating down the Niobrara, you'll see paper birch trees on the south side of the river valley due to the changes left by the last glaciers over South Dakota. His background as a big game hunting guide and a fisherman makes him the perfect guide for a hike, a trip down the river, or just a conversation around the campfire. Utilizing technology like GPS makes it possible to guide visitors without necessarily taking them himself, thus freeing time for other responsibilities.

Steve has an explicit focus on natural resource conservation. This is apparent in his land-management strategies. He has adapted a ranching style that emphasizes diverse pastures. In response to the question, "Is conservation of natural resources a factor in what you do?", he said:

"Look at my pastures. My grazing plan…you can't even tell anything's been out there. I'm not even running cattle this year. Part of the attraction is leaving this in a natural state. Bringing in some people allows me to do that. If I wasn't doing that, I'd have to be grazing that [the pasture] down… I'd be changing the speciation of my warm and cool season grasses. So [natural resource conservation] is definitely a driving force."

In general, Steve exhibits characteristics important of an entrepreneur. He's an innovator open to new ideas and interested in evolving his business.

For example, Steve and Niobrara Riverview Retreats host groups of entomologists, including individuals from the University of Nebraska-Lincoln. Through these interactions, Steve can explain the insect diversity on his ranch. Visiting entomologists have confirmed that the area is a great place to see and study certain insects. A wide diversity of dragonflies and damselflies, butterflies, and tiger beetles call the ranch home. Perhaps representing another opportunity, he is enrolled in a Conservation Reserve Program specific to pollinator habitat and will be planting in the fall of 2015.

The Niobrara contains more than 200 waterfalls in its 535 miles. Photo: Steve Hansen

Steve Hansen

Our Heritage Guest Ranch

JEAN NORMAN
Our Heritage Guest Ranch
Toadstool Road,
Crawford, NE 69339

www.vacation-ranch.com
308-430-1239

Activities: Natural horsemanship lessons and equine retreats, guided trail rides, Lakota vacations, ranch experiences, hiking, photography, fossil digs, art workshops

Customer base: Mostly visitors from the East or West coasts who are seeking the "real cowboy" experience; occasional European travelers; trail horse riders

Facilities/Capacity: Two new apartments in renovated horse stables, each with full bath and four beds each. The Bed & Breakfast Cabin is a full house with multiple bedrooms and baths available for guests.

Rates: Each vacation package has a set price with discounts provided for groups. The basic guest ranch experience, including meals, lodging, and regular activities, is $125 per person per day.

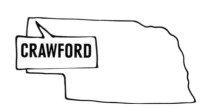

Jean Norman with her horses at Our Heritage Guest Ranch.

THE STORY

Our Heritage Guest Ranch is nestled in picturesque Pine Ridge country in the Panhandle of Nebraska. Owner Jean Norman is a fourth-generation rancher and caretaker of the land and has a wealth of experience and knowledge of the region. She's worked in various areas of tourism including as a tour guide and horse wrangler at nearby Fort Robinson State Park. Jean has been training horses since she was a teenager and today passes along natural horsemanship skills to visitors through retreats and multi-day riding experiences. In addition to natural veterinary practices, Jean is also involved with naturopathy and natural approaches to human health.

"

> I teach my guests how to become close to the land and appreciate the beauty and life here. They hike, bike, and ride horseback while filling their lungs with fresh air. The activities and surroundings create the connection with nature.

Jean works to tailor to her guests' interests by offering a number of themed activities. Most are geared toward groups of eight to twenty people. These include artist retreats, guided fossil digs, and several themed multi-day horseback expeditions. On Our Heritage's website, it reads:

"The Lakota Sioux Tour or the Pioneer Vacation are designed to be an educational step into the past. We have been working with a natural lifestyle for several years now in addition to working with nature in our ranching. Through this enriched lifestyle we have found out prior to our ancestors homesteading here that our land was used as a spiritual healing place by the Native Americans. We wish to honor both ancestries through these two packages."

A local woman educated by Lakota elders leads Jean's three-to-six-day Lakota journey. She introduces groups to the plants and animals of the area as well as Lakota culture, astrology, traditional cooking, and storytelling. This journey includes a sweat lodge, Tee Pee accommodations, and horseback riding instruction on Native American riding techniques. In June, groups ride to Fort Robinson to participate in the Annual Intertribal Pow Wow.

The Pioneer Vacation rides are three-to-five-day trips planned around particular community events. August's county fair provides a rodeo and a western dance. In July, expeditions take a trip to Chadron's Fur Trade Days and local Fourth of July celebrations. Guests can also plan their trips around the Intertribal Pow Wow, the high school rodeo, or shows at the Post Playhouse at Fort Robinson. Jean has shorter horseback expeditions, as well. She takes guests on horseback to nearby Toadstool Geological Park, the Hudson Meng archeological site, and the Drifter's Cookshack for dinner. Both the Lakota and Pioneer experiences require a group of ten to twenty individuals, and the schedule and activities depend on the group's preferences.

At the heart of each ride is an in-depth natural horsemanship training. Guests spend time getting to know their horse, brushing, maneuvering, and working with the animals on the ground. Jean said, "My job is to make sure that your relationship [with the horse] is going well."

"I start with the process, and I explain that horses mirror our inner-self. It's about energy work. Their instinct will exhibit to you what you are because they are able to read you instantaneously. They respond accordingly. "

Jean's natural approach to horsemanship, with its emphasis on relationships and interpersonal energy, has led to some transformational experiences for her guests. She reports that she's had a number of guests who've made important discoveries about themselves and their family situations via her unique training. She does a specific retreat with the American Competitive Trail Horse Association called Saved by the Love of Horses in which participants dive deep into holistic horse-care topics, from clicker training and sound therapy to search and rescue.

Guests enjoy bird songs and peaceful scenery in the Nebraska badlands.

The environment of the ranch alone is enough to spur personal discovery. Jean markets Our Heritage Guest Ranch as remote, scenic, and relaxing. She says on the website that "its seclusion is one of the attractive elements we have to offer. People enjoy their stay in the quiet atmosphere only disrupted by an occasional train. They get a true feel of how nature is at its best."

"Working with nature and not against nature has been instilled in the operation of this ranch throughout its history."

Jean likes to talk to guests about ranchers as conservationists, dispelling negative perceptions about agriculture in the state. She runs up to 500 cattle on her ranch, so naturally she starts by explaining herd management, grazing practices, and the benefits of grass-fed beef. Jean also teaches her guests about the ranch's method of water conservation via gravity-fed irrigation, a system of dykes and ditches modeled after traditional Native American techniques. She explains how these practices **24** create an important habitat for wildlife.

My great-grandparents, grandparents, and dad all took advantage of the land without going against it. We have to be good caretakers of the land in order to survive on it. If we ruin it, we ruin our livelihood.

Rich in geologic and western history, the area surrounding Our Heritage Guest Ranch includes many top Panhandle attractions. Toadstool National Park, the Hudson-Meng Bison Bone Bed, Agate Fossil Bed, and the Mammoth Museum are all part of the Fossil Freeway and all close. The Museum of the Fur Trade and Fort Robinson are also popular cultural and historical attractions. The Black Hills National Forest and Mount Rushmore are just two hours away in South Dakota.

Jean's guests often enjoy participating in the ranch's seasonal activities: fixing fences, haying, lambing, and calving. They are taking part in the real cowboy lifestyle. Guests can also participate in art workshops where they can work with photography, paint, and other mediums. Jean makes artistic cabinetry from recycled materials, and assists guests in making their own rustic, Western-style furniture.

Far from stoplights and big city chaos, a vacation at Our Heritage is a chance to connect with the picturesque landscape and intriguing heritage of northwest Nebraska.

Rock formations at Toadstool Geological Park.

HIGH PLAINS HOMESTEAD

MIKE AND LINDA KESSELRING
263 Sandcreek Road
Crawford, NE 69339
308-665-2592

www.highplainshomestead.com

Activities: Hunting, horseback riding, fossil hunting, mountain biking, birding, hiking

Facilities/Capacity: The High Plains Homestead is a beautifully rustic re-creation of an Old West town, featuring a school house, saloon, mercantile, post office, jail, and blacksmith shop. Individual lodging is available. At the center of "town" life is the Drifter's Cookshack, a restaurant featuring high-quality, home-cooked meals.

Lodging is six individual rooms with space for groups of up to 20 people total. Space for campers, tents, and horse boarding is also available.

Basic Rates: $68.50 per night, single occupancy. $10.50 per night for each additional room guest. Includes free breakfast, wireless internet, and swimming pool. Also free fossil hunting for beginners and parents with small children.

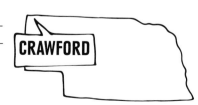

THE STORY

> We are western hospitality, cowboy cuisine, meat and potatoes kind of stuff. — Mike Kesselring

"Because of the incredibly low light pollution at High Plains Homestead, every night, the best show in the universe is visible from your front porch." – High Plains Homestead website

When one drives along a desolate dirt road in the high plains of northwestern Nebraska, High Plains Homestead appears like an oasis. The Old West outpost is located in the middle of the Oglala National Grasslands, an expanse of more than 90,000 acres of African-like savannahs. This prairie landscape intersects with nearby dramatic badlands

Guests can enjoy homemade meals at the Drifter Cookshack.

formations and the Pine Ridge buttes. After sixteen years of business, owners and Nebraska tourism veterans Mike and Linda Kesselring have seen a lot of repeat visitors—and for good reason. The couple works hard at creating a welcoming retreat. They embody western hospitality and greet all guests that come through the screen door like long-lost relatives.

At the heart of the High Plains Homestead is the Drifter Cookshack, a restored log cabin where guests eat and congregate and travelers stop in for breakfast, lunch, or dinner. But this isn't just any road food—it's all made by hand, including the bread and rolls. On a Friday or Saturday night, visitors can enjoy a classic cookout with steak, ribs, or salmon and occasionally bison, raised right there at the ranch. Collecting eggs for breakfast is a popular activity, especially among younger guests.

Many people make the journey through the dusty Nebraska Badlands specifically for Linda's famous pies. Her "Indian tacos" have even been featured on TV's Food Network. Beer and wine are available at the Cookshack and the Dirty Creek Saloon, another restored cabin just a few hundred feet away.

The Homestead is a unique concept: an Old West town in the middle of nowhere with no modern buildings in sight. The experience isn't so much about activities—although there's plenty to see and do—but about stepping into a place you've only read about or seen in movies. It has romantic western flair combined with the nostalgia of going home to grandma's house, said Mike. "It's got a family-oriented kind of feel. That's one of the strengths of a family-oriented business is you can provide something like that."

Mike and Linda represent the middle of three generations on the ranch. They started the operation with Mike's father in 1997. Mike remembers the family living in trailers along the river as they set the place up by deconstructing old homestead houses in the region and assembling them on their property. Mike was the first state chairman of the Nebraska

GO SEE ★

State Tourism Commission and continues to be an active promoter of tourism in the region. The High Plains Homestead is part of the Bridges to Buttes Scenic Byway, the Northwest Nebraska High Country group, and the Western Nebraska Tourism Coalition.

High Plains Homestead has a clearly defined mission statement on their website.

High Plains Homestead, LLC is a private, family owned business dedicated to providing all visitors and customers a quality, rural western experience through good food, hospitality, and education that is inviting, safe, fun, informative, and draws an appreciation for the area and the generations of people who have inhabited the NW Nebraska grasslands and badlands.

As far as education and interpretation of the natural surroundings, Mike and Linda are certainly capable regional guides. In his sixteen years in tourism, Mike's learned that "nobody wants to be beat on the head, but everyone wants to experience something new." Speaking specifically on grasslands conservation, he said, "It's about respect. And hopefully respect leads to that. I try to teach people that grass is so important." Sitting at the breakfast table, Mike pointed out the patch of bare ground across the road that somebody tried to till-up decades ago. It's never grown back.

"None of this, including the people, would not be here if not for the grass. Taking care of that has to be number one.

You can teach people the heritage and the story that came behind that. Hopefully that'll bring a new respect and a new appreciation. I think that's the start of things. That's what we're trying to do here, rather than hold a grass seminar."

Sitting on the porch, Mike can identify many of the birds that pass through. On the website, they list an extensive list of bird species in the area: Eagles, hawks, owls, turkeys, doves, woodpeckers, swallows, magpies, larks, and finches. Pine-dependent bird species also abound here: Lewis' woodpecker, pinyon jay, dark-eyed junco, sage thrasher, western tanager, yellow-rumped warbler, Swainson's thrush, solitary vireo, pygmy nuthatch, red crossbill, and the canyon-adapted cordilleran flycatcher.

The land around the Homestead is rich with the fossil remains of the early Cenozoic mammals. Just three miles northwest is the Hudson-Meng Education and Research Center, an interpretative center on top of the largest extinct bison bonebed in the world. Just west of Crawford, Fort Robinson's Trailside Museum features a unique fossil exhibit called the "Clash of the Titans." These fighting mammoths frozen in time were unearthed in nearby Sioux County. Other regional attractions including the Agate Fossil Beds, the Wildcat Hills, and the Hot Springs Mammoth Site in South Dakota are all part of a group tourism effort called the Fossil Freeway.

Mike also works closely with the Northwest Nebraska High Country group, a sort of rural chamber of commerce. The group has twenty-five members that include guest ranches, country stores, and other privately owned businesses catering to tourists. The group began more than a decade ago when a handful of developing businesses saw a common goal in promoting the region. Mike said at the time, the idea of mutual promotion was controversial and new. But, he said, people came around when they realized their success was tied to the success of others and the region. "No one is going to go anywhere and stay one place on a vacation. It just isn't going to happen," he said, "So you let the region work for you."

Guests at the High Plains Homestead spend most of their time enjoying simple pleasures: Eating home-cooked meals, seeing the stars, playing with the cats, and chatting on the front porch. Mike says most of his visitors are just there to relax and experience something different. **31**

"Ecotourism is a term that is something we put on our brochure to communicate to the city people with, so we have a common language. People used to call that country living; now they call it ecotourism."

Mike says people in his part of the state raise their own food, save water, recycle materials, and even install "curly light bulbs" because it's their way of life to conserve scarce resources. "In this part of the country, **32** that's just how we've lived from day one." After years of interactions,

his approach to conservation-education is much more casual than what you'd find at a state or national park, but perhaps more memorable. Mike calls it a "subtle invitation to love the land" that comes about through stories and human connections.

DOUBLE R GUEST RANCH

PAT BRIDGES
Double R Guest Ranch
86091 Double R Drive
Mullen, NE 69152

http://www.sandhilldoublerranch.com
866-217-2042

Activities: Hunting, fishing, ice-fishing, hiking, bird-watching, star-gazing, ranch tours and activities, in-season cattle roundups and brandings, blue rock shooting, wildflower identification, wildlife viewing

Customer Base: More than half of visitors are vacationers from out of state and overseas. Many repeat visitors come from Nebraska cities and towns. The average stay is 2-3 days.

Facilities/Capacity: 16 people; 25 max; three cabins in a secluded, wooded area within a century-old Ponderosa pine forest and a large spring-fed lake nearby. There are no individual rooms, the spaces are intended for groups. All are furnished and include kitchenettes, cookware, utensils, and appliances. Linens and bedding are also provided.

Rates: Two persons start at $75 per night.
Each additional person, age 10 and older, is an additional $30 per night.

Pat Bridges on her family's ranch.

THE STORY

Pat Bridges and her husband Jim bought the Roth family ranch in the Nebraska Sandhills in 1984. They started the Double R Guest Ranch as a complementary business to their cattle operation. Pat's grandfather was the first and only doctor in the area when the family arrived as homesteaders in 1908. In the years Jim and Pat have lived here, they've worked to keep up the historical buildings, build new cabins, plant hundreds of trees, and maintain the biodiversity of their grassland home—all labors of love.

"I try to emphasize the conservation that has taken place and how the rancher takes such good care of their land; how they move the cattle around, grazing the pastures to extend the usefulness of the grasses."

The drive to Double R Guest Ranch is along one of the most scenic and least populated stretches of highway in the state, Highway 97, connecting North Platte to Valentine. The Bridges' property includes three big lakes and is a working cattle ranch. Since Jim died a few years back, a neighbor takes care of the livestock business. Pat dedicates most of her time to hosting visitors from around the country and the world. She's put herself on the map by tirelessly marketing the natural beauty and isolation that makes her place special.

36 Pat is an attentive and fascinating host. She worked for decades in law as a legal secretary, court clerk, court reporter, and clerk-magistrate. Her second career was at the world-renowned Sandhills Golf Course and it was here, through her interactions with visitors, that she came up with the tourism concept. "I just realized how special this area was," she said. "People came in from all over to the Sandhills Golf Course, and that's all they could talk about." She added, "I just thought it was stupid to have all these buildings and no one using them." The buildings include her grandparents' original 1908 sod house, a restored one-room school house, a little gift shop that was originally a doctor's office, stables and a barn, a calving shed and shop, and a wooden cabin near a fishing lake.

Hunting, fishing, and family gatherings are the bread and butter of her business. Most visitors stay two or three nights. She said after fourteen years, the word is out and she is "as busy as she wants to be." She sends guests to the Merritt Reservoir and to Valentine for day trips, but she says, "Most of the time, the guests come to relax. They think they're going to do this or that and when they get here, they just unwind and enjoy the surroundings."

Pat recently bought an all-terrain vehicle (ATV) with the thought of providing ranch tours to visitors. While this is an opportunity to expand her ecotourism activities via an interpretive tour, she says she may be "getting too old" to be the one out driving! Although she can arrange for planned activities, Pat's enterprise is based on family-friendly lodging in a beautiful, isolated place. Her guests have the opportunity to appreciate and explore the pristine grassy sandhills reaching out in every direction.

I don't have structured activities, and I think that's okay. It wouldn't be for everybody, but being the sole provider here, there is no way that I can do a lot of the things I would like to. I'm doing what I can. It seems to satisfy most of the guests. They always find a way to entertain themselves.

Horses are a passion for Pat. The opportunity to ride horses on the open range has attracted many visitors to her land over the years. Pat says she is happy to accommodate those who bring their own horses and ride them on her land. Unfortunately, her business can no longer offer horses or organized trail rides to guests. Pat doesn't have the necessary help for such a program and she's grown weary of the liability issues involved. **37**

For more than ten years, she has actively campaigned for state laws to address the horseback riding statutes and risk for landowners.

On her website, Pat markets the many bird species that visit the ranch: Sharp-tail grouse, ring-necked pheasants, long-billed curlew, pelicans, swans, blue herons, terns, many ducks and geese, and many other grassland birds. She also promotes nature photography as an activity:

"At dusk the hills are alive with their deepest shades of green making early evening the best time to get the beautiful shadows on the hills, and to capture the clouds in all their glory. The myriad wildflowers will have their best colorings at dusk with some closing up and some just beckoning. At the close of the day, the howl of the coyotes, and the yipping of their little ones, may remind you that Mother Nature is on continual watch over every creature under the sky!"

Pat is a strong advocate for rural tourism and ecotourism in her native Sandhills. She's an active member of the Sandhills Journey Scenic Byways group and has been part of initiatives to bring artists-in-residency to ranches along the Sandhills Byway. She also encourages her neighbors to explore tourism as an option for additional ranch income, but warns that hosting visitors is a time-consuming pursuit. Since she made this her full-time job, Pat says the Double R has grown considerably over the years. "I was just doing it off the cuff before I quit working at the golf club," she said. Pat has worked hard, successfully turning her family's home into a unique Sandhills destination. "I don't recommend you doing it if you don't have somebody there to answer the phone," she said. "You have to be attentive to business at all times."

Uncle Buck's Lodge

MARILYN RHOADS
Uncle Buck's Lodge
455 Brewster Ave.
Brewster, NE 68821

www.unclebuckslodge.com
308-547-2210

Services: Lodge accommodations, restaurant/bar, corporate retreats, events, hunting, canoeing/kayaking/tanking down the North Loup River, native/medicinal plant walk

Customer Base: Mostly summer traffic, family reunions; turkey hunters.

Facilities/Capacity: A big lodge, restaurant, access to the family ranch, which includes a long stretch of the Loup River. The restaurant, western bar and dining room are open for guests and special events. Can accommodate up to 24 visitors in eight double rooms and a large bunkroom. One room is handicap-accessible.

Rates: Rooms run from $45 (shared bath) to $75 (private bath) a night.

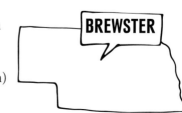

THE STORY

Located in the Nebraska Sandhills, Uncle Buck's Lodge is part of the Rhoads family ranch near Brewster. The ranch, comprising more than 10,000 acres, has been in the family since 1881. Marilyn Rhoads manages the daily operations of the lodge while her husband and daughter work primarily in the cattle ranch side of the business. Their pitch to the prospective visitor via their website:

"Step away from the crowd and come to Uncle Buck's Lodge, a ten thousand-acre working cattle ranch where you can roam free and discover that cowboy in you."

The lodge itself is a large building on the edge of the town of Brewster. The interior is reminiscent of an old western saloon complete with a long bar. A multitude of mounted animals and cowboy art, textiles, and family memorabilia decorate the walls. Each room is named for the historic families of Brewster and is decorated with photographs and artifacts that tell the stories of these families.

When Marilyn's mother was alive, she could be found quilting up on a balcony overlooking the lodge's Great Room with its large fireplace and floor-to-ceiling windows. Her quilting space remains a cozy corner and many of her tapestries line the walls. From here, one has a great view of the North Loup River and the open range beyond.

The tiny village of Brewster, population eighteen, is very sleepy, the majority of its roads left unpaved. Downtown is all but empty except for an antiques business, lending itself to a general feeling of friendly isolation. On their website, Uncle Buck's presents the appeal:

"Kick back and enjoy the peace and quiet of the pristine Nebraska Sandhills, or do some hunting, fishing or canoeing, or saddle up and join us in the work of an old-time cattle ranch. Uncle Buck's welcomes your family, friends and colleagues to the ranching life with a heart as big as the Nebraska sky."

Brewster and Uncle Buck's are located just off Nebraska Highway 91, part of the Loup Rivers Scenic Byway. The Byway is an organized group of communities and individuals who work to market the region through creative means. The Junk Jaunt, a huge, multi-community garage sale, is a popular summer event. There are multiple attractions along the Loup Rivers Scenic Byway including a new network of butterfly gardens open to the public.

Marilyn said most of her guests come to "get away" and that perhaps the most popular "activity" is socializing indoors on one of the big, comfortable couches. But when guests want to venture outside, she can arrange for horseback riding in the area. Marilyn also organizes hunting activities through a nearby outfitter. Guests can take canoes out on the North Loup. She also sends guests across the street to a goat farm and country store with homemade goat milk ice cream. But the central activity offered to guests is an experience on the family's ranch.

Each spring the Rhoads brand calves in a traditional manner. They round them up with horses, rope them, and use hot irons. This event attracts a small number of visitors, usually city-dwellers who are curious about ranch life. The ranch heritage is central to what the Rhoads do. As the website explains:

> It is our hope to keep the ranching tradition alive and preserve its heritage and culture. We founded Uncle Buck's as a way to diversify our operation and share the ranching experience with our many guests.

Like other guest ranches, Uncle Buck's provides a look into rural living and ranch culture. For many visitors, this is a way to connect with family heritage—what one's parents or grandparents did—and usually a lifestyle radically different than the norm.

"Our repeat guests tell us they enjoy a way of life that has disappeared in many parts of the country."

The family is proud to manage the ranch using holistic, chemical-free management practices. Their website states, "These practices optimize game production and benefit the ecological health of our land and water resources." The Rhoads family's explicit focus on natural practices makes their ranch and lodge a great combination of ecotourism and agritourism.

Bike tourists take a break at Uncle Buck's. Photo: Marilyn Rhoades

"A lot of times people just like to go observe ranch life…calving, branding cattle, hearing about rotational grazing, that sort of thing," she said. The Rhoads family is proud to raise hormone-free beef on organic grass. Marilyn said she was at first surprised to learn visitors cared about their ranch practices. "I think a lot of the city people, they want to know where their food comes from," said Marilyn.

44   Hunting is also promoted as a natural activity. On the website

it reads, "Uncle Buck's Outfitters manages these abundant lands for the exclusive, private use of its clients, practicing chemical-free, and Holistic Resource Management methods to assure adequate cover for optimal game production."

The hunters also come for something else. Camaraderie, old-time hospitality, and a special kind of Sandhills restfulness.

Turkey hunting is a big draw. Uncle Buck's has hosted hunters from across the United States and many foreign countries. Bird watching is an emerging activity. In the past, Marilyn has had self-guided groups of birders stay at the lodge, but she does not currently provide any specific birding activities.

Seasonally in the lodge, you might find wreaths of wild begonias or western yarrow adorning the halls. Cat tail pollen bread, deep-fried yucca blossoms, lambs quarter casserole, rose hip jelly—Marilyn has cooked all these menu items with wild edibles from her land. In the past, she held a yearly wildflower walk and wild edible meal for a small number of guests. Uncle Buck's is a great place to connect with land and relax with the family.

45

BIG BLUE RANCH & LODGE

SCOTT AND BILLIE KAY BODIE
Big Blue Ranch & Lodge
70804 608th Ave
Burchard, NE 68232

http://bigblueranch.com
402-865-4335

Activities: Lodging, fishing, hunting, horseback riding, hiking, bird watching, photography opportunities, and ranch lifestyle.

Customer base: High season is from April to October. Nature and wildlife enthusiasts; families with children who come for the weekend; father and son fishing trips; romantic getaways; family reunions and hunting trips. Average stay is two nights or more.

Facilities/capacity: The spacious lodge is built as two mirror-image suites. Each suite has two bedrooms which comfortably sleep six people. The suites can be joined by opening double doors, accommodating 12 people total.

Both suites in the lodge have full kitchens. One side is fully wheelchair accessible. Charcoal grills are also available. A large covered porch on each side of the lodge provides views of the lake and native grasslands. The lake has been stocked for over 50 years with large mouth bass, blue gill, crappie and catfish. It has a 60-foot dock and a picnic table, boats and a canoe to enjoy.

Rates: Starting at $200 for two people in a full suite. $25 for each additional person, including children. Fishing is included in the price. Horseback riding, hunting, and bird watching are add-ons.

BREWSTER

THE STORY

Scott and Billie Kay Bodie started Big Blue Ranch & Lodge in 2007 on Scott's family land near Burchard, about an hour and a half southeast of Lincoln. The working cattle ranch stands out as an ecological gem in the rolling hills of nature's original tall grass prairie. Its groves of trees, large ponds, and restored grasslands are unique in southeastern Nebraska, and so, too, is the Bodie family.

Before settling on the ranch, Scott and Billie Kay lived and traveled all over the world. They started raising a young family in Brazil. But the more people they met, the more they realized that they came from a truly special place. They write on their website, "After meeting and talking with people from all walks of life, we realized a lot of them don't know much about cattle ranches, and they are often interested in learning more about real cowboys, their horses, and the whole ball of wax. We decided to share this outdoor experience with others and started Big Blue Ranch & Lodge."

Billie Kay and Scott are sustainability-minded landowners. Their family has worked for generations to improve the sustainability and diversity of their pastures with carefully-controlled rotational grazing, by inter-seeding beneficial legumes, and through controlled burning.

They also care for sections of virgin tallgrass native prairie and hedgerows of trees planted by the original homesteaders (for guests interested in that period of history, the Homestead National Monument is just forty minutes away).

The open prairie, woodlands, lakes, and draws are preserved and protected as habitats for many kinds of wildlife including: deer, turkey, raccoon, badger, ground squirrel, ground hog, red squirrel, coyote, skunk, fox, bobcat, shrew, fire flies, toads, leopard frogs, and bull frogs. Many types of birds, including waterfowl, birds of prey, and the famed greater prairie chicken, are also found on the Big Blue Ranch.

The ranch itself has been honored with a number of conservation awards such as the Rangeland Conservation Award from the Lower Big Blue Natural Resources District. The University of Nebraska holds an annual class on the ranch, taught by Dr. Walter Schacht, to help students develop ranch management plans for a class project.

The decision to build the lodge on their land and offer hospitality to visitors was an effort to diversify and support more family members on the ranch. One daughter, Anne, her husband Rob, and their children all help with various aspects of the lodge and ecotourism business. Scott and Billie Kay say they

Guests fish at the lake, which can be seen from the lodge. Photo: Billie Kay Bodie

find it rewarding to share what they've developed with other families and especially kids.

"We always tell people to go outside at sunset and listen for coyotes howling, for the great horned owl, for turkeys…

High school seniors have come out here who've never seen the

Milky Way or a shooting star. They're excited. That's the fun of it. We enjoy visiting with them. That's the joy of it."

The log lodge they built is a stunning place, featuring red oak hardwood floors and knotty pine walls, stone fireplaces, Italian-style red clay tile work, and tasteful western design. The Bodies paid attention to every detail, importing white cedar logs from Canada, custom-building the comfortable log beds, and getting the view of the lake just right. From the spacious back porch, one is perfectly situated for taking in spectacular Nebraska sunsets over the 20-acre lake. Their website reads:

"**This Nebraska guest ranch combines the rustic beauty of yesterday with modern amenities. It's the cabin by the lake that you've always wanted.**"

The Bodies enjoy interacting with all kinds of people, and their international backgrounds make them especially comfortable playing host to global guests.

"**We had some guests who came here from Italy. They could hardly speak English. They were going to stay two nights and instead they stayed three. They were thrilled to be here on a cattle ranch, in the country. Here they had the vastness, the space, the freedom, the natural beauty.**"

The Bodie family seeks to promote Big Blue Ranch and Lodge as a deluxe ranch experience. Burchard's proximity to Lincoln, Omaha, and Kansas City means that they are not far from major airports. Yet Big Blue Ranch and Lodge is isolated and "country" enough to appeal to visitors

looking for something different.

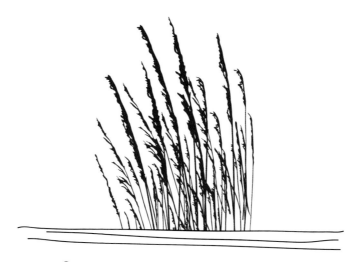

SHEEP WAGON HIDEOUTS

JIM AND LORA O'ROURKE
Sheep Wagon Hideouts
61 Country Club Road
Chadron, NE 69337

http://www.sheepwagonhideouts.com
308-432-5954

Activities: Unique lodging in historic sheepwagons, camping, fishing, nature walks, historical land use discussions, demonstrations of range management practices.

Customer base: Infrequent guests concentrated in the summer months.

Facilities/capacity: Three sheepwagons are dispersed among the ponderosa pine forest on the O'Rourke family's RuJoDen Ranch. Wagons are accessible by foot, situated up to a mile from the parking area. Water for drinking and bathing, a cooler, linens, towels, cookware, utensils, lanterns, and a porta-potty are provided. Guests bring their own food to cook on the woodstove.

CHADRON

Rates: $80 a night.

THE STORY

Degree-holding, land management specialists with fascinating backgrounds, Jim and Lora O'Rourke are the perfect guides for the unique ecology of northwestern Nebraska's rangelands (open country used for grazing or hunting). Lora is retired from the U.S. Forest Service while Jim is a retired professor with a distinguished international career. Both speak with detailed authority about the family's land, the RuJoDen Ranch, a stunning collage of timbered ridges and diverse grasslands just outside of Chadron.

Jim came to Chadron State College as an agriculture professor in 1988 and soon after founded the college's range management program. Previously, he worked for the U.S. Forest Service and Bureau of Land Management on private ranches in Wyoming, Colorado, Arizona, and New Mexico, and taught range management at Utah State University. He worked eight years in range management in Tanzania, Morocco, and several other African countries. The couple worked together in Nigeria before moving to Jim's family's land in Nebraska. Now retired from teaching, Jim focuses considerable energy on his work with the Society for Range Management and the International Rangeland Congresses. Various leadership positions continue to take Jim all over the world to speak and consult on range management.

Jim and Lora both come from genuine cowboy roots. Jim's grandfather worked on the famous Spade Ranch in the Nebraska Sandhills and bought the RuJoDen in 1950. For twenty-five years, the land was grazed by a free-ranging herd of horses. Jim explains the steps he and Lora took to restore the RuJoDen Ranch back to permanent grass, forb, shrub and tree vegetation. Where nine pastures existed are now nineteen, allowing for an intensive cattle grazing rotation.

You've got to graze it, but you've got to graze it quick, then get off of it and let the plants recover.

"Cattle graze no more than twenty days out of the year per pasture; the remaining 345 days are for wildlife," explains Jim. He proudly showcases the diverse collection of native grasses and forbs that have reappeared through the use of this system: little and big bluestem, sideoats grama, green needlegrass, soapweed, prairie wildrose, dotted gay-

Guests stay in restored sheep wagons on the RuJoDen Ranch. Herders would use these wagons in the western United States to protect themselves from the elements.

feather, shell-leaf penstemon, and prairie coneflower, to name just a few.

"Our concept on improved pastures is if you've got a diversity of an acre here and two acres there – you've got diversity. It's not on a square foot scale, but on a landscape scale. Animals can go from one area to the other for whatever is important for them. It also allows for a lot better grazing management. You can concentrate on one species, to hurt it or to save it, and you can graze it in different seasons. You can really create some great biodiversity."

"It took a hell of a lot of years to get that diversity," says Jim. He's glad to go into detail or leave you to explore on your own, if you prefer.

"Nature walks, historical land use discussions or demonstrations of sustainable use of rangeland are available depending on your desires… or you can simply enjoy the

quiet and solitude of a stay in a sheep wagon."

The Pine Ridge landscape is beautiful and varied. Nearby, the White River valley creates rough, steep terrain dissected by deep drainage ways. On the ranch, there are riparian areas along Chadron Creek as well as rocky ridges dominated by ponderosa pine, scattered Rocky Mountain juniper, and stands of mountain mahogany.

The major appeal of staying at Sheepwagon Hideouts is spending the night in an historic sheep wagon. Similar to a covered wagon, the sheep wagon was designed to provide shelter, heat, mobility, and storage for sheep herders on the open rangelands of the western United States. Jim and Lora have a growing collection of sheep wagons which they love to talk about. Three of them are available for guests, situated on the edges of the ranch amidst the peaceful ponderosas.

A single traveler or a couple will be cozy in the wagons. They are approximately 11.5 feet long and 6.5 feet wide. They include a lofted bed, benches, a table, shelves, and an antique cook stove. Guests can enjoy the simple pleasures of cooking their own meal on the stove, stargazing, and snuggling up to the sounds of the great outdoors.

In the last century, the woods were logged with horses, leaving well-defined trails great for hiking up the canyons to the top of the ridge. On a walk-about, it's possible to spot plenty of wildlife: white-tailed and mule deer, coyote, fox, raccoon, and bobcats. Elk, bighorn sheep, and mountain lion migrate through the property, as well. It's also possible to spot plenty of birds including Merriam's turkey, sharp-tail grouse, mourning dove, pheasant, pygmy nuthatch, great horned owl, red-tail hawk, king fisher, blue heron, and many more.

Riparian areas (the spaces between land and river) are managed for regeneration of native woody species, and Lora and Jim have expanded these areas with tree plantings and drip-irrigation. They take this major land restoration project very seriously. Jim says they've experimented with around eighty species and have hand-planted nearly 10,000 trees to date. A fish pond is available for guests, stocked with rainbow trout for catch and release fishing. Fishing costs are discounted for guests

Jim O'Rourke out and about as storm clouds roll in.

staying the night in a sheep wagon.

Jim and Lora are also collectors of horse-drawn farm machinery. Jim takes visitors on tours through a vast graveyard of rusting implements, each with a particular and fascinating history that demonstrates the ingenuity of the pioneers who first ranched in the area.

There is hunting at RuJoDen, but the O'Rourkes only allow one hunt per species per season for turkeys, white tail, and mule deer. Those who do hunt enjoy coming back year after year to their special spot. "We get a lot of people who are repeat, who bring their kids for the first time hunting experience," said Jim. All hunting includes the non-guided use of both private and adjacent U.S. Forest Service public property. The sheep wagons are located in the heart of turkey and deer habitat and conveniently close to public lands, allowing for large areas of open access.

Whether hunting, fishing, seeing rangeland management in action, or just relaxing in the comforts of a century-old sheep wagon, Sheepwagon Hideouts is a spot like no other.

ECOTOURISM & SAVING THE GREAT PLAINS

GRASSLANDS

"Everywhere, as far as the eye could reach, there was nothing but rough, shaggy, red grass, most of it as tall as I. ... As I looked about me I felt that the grass was the country, as the water is the sea." — Willa Cather, *My Ántonia*

America's central grassland, originally stretching from Illinois to the Rockies and from north Texas to mid-Manitoba, astonished early travelers. Many could not get comfortable in its vastness and lack of visible landmarks, and few could resist using the "sea of grass" metaphor. They were amazed at the profusion of its wildlife. But even then it took the first true field botanists, among them Roscoe Pound of later Harvard Law fame, to discover that each small patch of prairie typically contained 150 or more different species of grasses and forbs.

This prairie has now mostly disappeared. It was plowed under to seed fields of corn, soybeans, and wheat. Only the shortgrass prairie, beginning at roughly the 100th meridian and extending to the foothills of the Rockies, survives in large intact areas. But it is under terrible threat.

The shortgrass prairie continues to be plowed up and "developed" at a great pace, its very lack of cities and super-highways making it an inviting target. Planners for the Keystone XL oil pipeline routed their project through the region, and the Nebraska Public Power District intends to build a huge high-voltage transmission line right across some of the most pristine and fragile terrain in the Sandhills. The plough-up accelerated when demand for corn for ethanol and other factors sent corn, soybean, and wheat prices surging, so land even recently deemed too marginal for row-crop production was planted to corn. One estimate suggested that South Dakota alone lost 250,000 acres of virgin prairie to row crops each year. Then when crop prices sag, as inevitably they do in the agricultural cycle, the new fields may remain unplanted, but the ploughed-up prairie doesn't return – its profusion of grasses and forbs are gone, the grassland destroyed. Replanting a *prairie* and not just a grass field is difficult and expensive work, as the folks at Prairie Plains Research Institute in Aurora, Nebraska, world-class prairie restorers, know. In the plough-up as elsewhere, most threats to biodiversity flow not from inadequate biological knowledge, but rather from *failed political and economic institutions that persistently undervalue landscape and bio-diversity.*

Why should we care about this grassland? After all, this is "the Big Empty," that mind-numbingly tedious region through which one has to drive to get to someplace interesting and noteworthy. Today it is known as fly-over country, an area conveniently forgotten during the in-flight movie. A 2008 *New York Times* article noted that the Nebraska "sandhills [have been] good for little more than hunting and grazing since forever...."

Yet ignorance hardly justifies neglect. It turns out that the earth's great grasslands, such as the Mongolian high plain, the African savanna, and our Great Plains, are regions of abundant biodiversity. As already noted, the American prairie displays a highly complicated botany. North America's most endangered mammal, the black-footed ferret, is a grasslands denizen. The Nebraska Sandhills, dismissed by the *Times* writer, is a fragile and unique ecosystem, the largest collection of stable dunes on the continent and home to some 230 species of birds and dozens of wildflower species. Dragonflies abound. When the sandhill cranes make their annual migration from the southwestern United States to their breeding grounds in the Arctic, they stop along a short stretch of the Platte River. Here they remain for a month or longer, convening in the hundreds of thousands to refuel for the rest of the trip. It turns out "the Big Empty," even the depleted Platte, is critical to maintaining biodiversity.

In 2005 four biologists reported a study in *Ecology Letters* of the world's 810 ecoregions (smaller-scale sub-categories nested within the thirteen recognized biomes or large ecosystems); they ranked how endangered each ecoregion is. Their conclusion: "temperate grasslands, savannas, and shrublands" are the most endangered environments on earth. There are certainly other regions – Madagascar, the Amazon basin, the coral reef off New Guinea – in urgent need of protection, but one of the most abused areas is right here in the center of our country.

So if the remaining North American grasslands are worth saving, what can be done? One approach is to have federal or state governments purchase landscape-scale properties. But the political culture and chronically strained budgets make this outcome unlikely. A second approach is for private non-governmental organizations, like The Nature Conservancy or Audubon Society, to purchase lands and remove them from

production agriculture. Such purchases save small and highly critical parcels, for which we also should be extremely grateful, but limited resources applied to a terrain this vast render the effort inherently modest in scope. New strategies, complementary to the first two, seem needed.

Ecotourism represents a third approach, a highly promising development with some novel, even counter-intuitive elements that is just now emerging. This approach starts by recognizing two hard realities: 1) most of the surviving Great Plains grasslands is privately owned; in Nebraska, for example, approximately ninety-three percent of the land is private; and 2) most current landowners, especially ranchers, adhere to a cattle-based western culture that is often not friendly to environmentalists and other perceived outsiders. However, they also see themselves as the inheritors and stewards of beautiful land that has often been in their family for several generations. The ecotourism approach seeks to turn these realities into positives by establishing private-market incentives for landowners to undertake conservation themselves. *Rather than excluding ranchers from conservation (as the first two approaches tend to do), this approach seeks to enlist them as the active, indeed crucial, agents in saving the biodiversity of the grasslands.* **61**

The logic of how ecotourism promotes conservation is simple. Ranchers and other landowners must provide protected habitat and sufficient wildlife – a meaningful environmental experience – to attract ecotourists. Ecotourists then spend money for access, lodging, food, guides, tours, and other services offered by ecotourism providers. Ranchers and landowners therefore have an economic incentive and reap an economic reward for maintaining habitat and protecting wildlife that attract ecotourists. The resulting flow of new dollars into the area spreads the economic stimulus to nearby communities, creating jobs and new business opportunities and giving community residents a stake in ecotourism and conservation, as well.

The origins of this new approach lie across the ocean in Namibia. This African country – unlike nearly all of its sub-Saharan neighbors – has experienced a tremendous *increase* in the numbers of all its wildlife species: more elephants, more kudu, more ostrich, more giraffe, more leopard, even more cheetahs. It achieved this result by making wildlife pay for local landowners. Namibia has two main types of landowners aside from the national government: communal (or tribal) and private.

The changes were simple but fundamental: 1) ownership of wildlife

was privatized, so that communal or private landowners rather than the state now owns and can benefit from wildlife on their property;[1] and 2) the state encouraged and in some cases required the establishment of nature conservancies, that is, communal and multi-farmer associations that manage wildlife jointly across their properties; the change forced an increase in the scale over which private wildlife is managed. The new rights were first granted to white farmers by the apartheid regime in 1967 and were extended to communal (tribal) lands by the black-majority government in 1996.[2]

The results have been impressive. The Namibian cattle farmer or local commune got new sources of income in trophy-hunting fees, meat sales, and, of increasing importance, revenues from wildlife viewing, photographic safaris, and lodges. Wildlife, instead of being pests and competitors with livestock for valuable grass, became an *asset* to farmers. Poaching has been nearly eliminated (wildlife is too valuable in attracting tourists to poach), and animal numbers have soared. Cattle (or goat) farming typically continues alongside the increasing wildlife, even coexisting with predators. *Most importantly, a country dominated by cattle and goat farmers who once despised wildlife has been transformed into a society highly conscious of its value and hence protective of the nation's wildlife.*

Can these ideas, suitably tailored for our own context, work to save American grasslands? There are many obstacles in applying them here: the so-called "North American model" of wildlife; entrenched bureaucracies, both private and public, which feel threatened; federal policies which subsidize commodity agriculture and provide little support for conservation; and most important, the culture of American ranching, which like its (former) Namibian counterpart, sees reducing wildlife as necessary to raising cattle.

But there are highly encouraging signs, as well. There are crusty old Sandhills ranchers who suffer the stresses of rising land taxes and high feed (corn) prices and so are attracted to having their land – their primary asset – provide an additional revenue source. Because it feels less

---

1. Ownership rights are complex, with the degrees of ownership varying by species, which are categorized into huntable game (such as springbok and oryx) or protected species (giraffe, roan) or specially-protected species (elephant, rhino), and by farm category (a fully game-proofed fence on private land versus a livestock fence only). Landowner rights and control over use are strongest for huntable game, less so for protected species, and much less so for specially-protected species.

2. An action plan for "Private Protected Areas" was approved at the 2005 (Durban) ICUN World Parks Conference.

like they are betraying their forebears, they like the idea that they could do conservation and ecotourism in combination with traditional cattle ranching. And some of the younger rancher generation are excited by the new opportunities to connect with the outside world, even with parts as remote as Namibia, to do conservation while making a profit. Perhaps ecotourism can provide a new revenue stream, a new way to help private landowners retain their land, pay their taxes, and persuade their children to move back home from Denver or Chicago. If so, it would have the additional benefit of creating incentives promoting private-lands conservation because ecotourists want to see wildlife, biodiversity, and uncluttered landscapes. They may become the new conservationists of the Plains.

Ecotourism sites provide places to walk, hike, camp, photograph, observe, learn, and reflect upon the wondrous natural environment that is the Great Plains. Some sites also offer opportunities to engage more deeply by volunteering or participating in programs that support and sustain this precious legacy. The kind of ecotourism we encourage is an experience of nature that is powerful for the individual and caring of the land. In this sense we seek low-volume, high-value tourism that is high-impact for the people and low-impact for the land.

While environmentalists and activists and scholars have been exploring models of ecotourism as one of the possibilities for supporting habitat and wildlife conservation, especially in areas where most of the land is privately owned, *private entrepreneurs are already building ecotourism on their own lands*. That's the real importance of this Guide, highlighting some of the heroes on the ground. They and many others in the for-profit sector, in non-profit organizations, and elsewhere are already doing it. We believe the future health of the Great Plains grasslands may well depend on their success. As private businesses, they must be profitable to survive; for the rest of us grasslands-lovers, their businesses must be profitable so the grasslands will survive.

Time to go! See you on the prairie!

The Great Plains Ecotourism Coalition is committed to promoting environmental conservation and building thriving communities through nature-based tourism in the Great Plains. The Coalition includes both non-profit and for-profit members.

The Coalition works to:

• Connect nature-based entrepreneurs with one another, creating opportunities for collaboration, learning, and cooperation.

• Market the region to ecotourists in the United States and beyond through targeted and creative advertising campaigns.

• Share information about ecotourism with participating members through a website, social media, and small conferences.

• Undertake or commission studies and research on ecotourism-related topics of substantial interest to members and ecotourists.

• Disseminate useful and reliable information of relevance to members.

• Engage in other activities to promote ecotourism in the Great Plains with the Coalition members' support.

More about the Coalition and the Center's Ecotourism work at go.unl.edu/ecotourism

Follow the Coalition on Twitter @GreatPlains or on Facebook at facebook.com/VisitThePrairie

Coalition Members

Double R Guest Ranch

GRAND ISLAND
NEBRASKA

Convention & Visitors Bureau

High Plains Homestead

 Homestead National
Monument of America

 Loup Rivers Scenic
Byway

NEBRASKA
Sustainable Agriculture Society

Niobrara River Retreats

Our Heritage Guest Ranch

Prairie Plains Resource Institute

IAIN NICOLSON Audubon
CENTER AT ROWE SANCTUARY

Sheepwagon Hideouts

Southern Plains
Land Trust

SPRING CREEK PRAIRIE Audubon CENTER

Switzer Ranch/Calamus Outfitters

The Joslyn Institute for Sustainable Communities

The Nature Conservancy

Protecting nature. Preserving life.

THE WILLA CATHER FOUNDATION

UNCLE BUCK'S LODGE

BREWSTER ★ NEBRASKA

UNIVERSITY
OF
NEBRASKA
STATE MUSEUM

School of Natural Resources

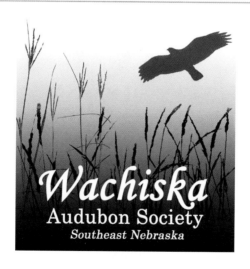

Wachiska
Audubon Society
Southeast Nebraska

Ecotourism Poster series

Twelve posters depicting the beauty of Nebraska were designed for the Center for Great Plains Studies by Lincoln, Neb., artist and Center Communications Coordinator Katie Nieland. Based on the 1930s Works Progress Administration's National Parks prints, they focus on the stunning landscapes and creatures found in the Plains.

The posters serve as a kick-off project for the Great Plains Ecotourism Coalition. The Center's goal is to see the poster set travel the state to encourage viewers to visit the natural wonders found in the Great Plains.

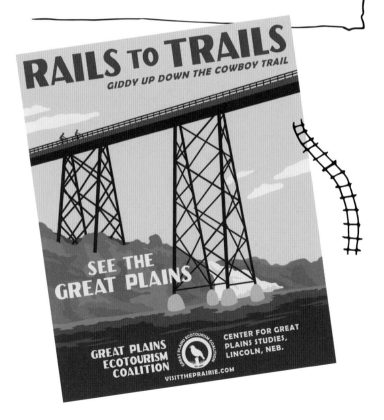

FOSSIL FREEWAY

TAKE A TRIP BACK IN TIME

SEE THE GREAT PLAINS

GREAT PLAINS
ECOTOURISM
COALITION

CENTER FOR GREAT
PLAINS STUDIES,
LINCOLN, NEB.

BISON REBIRTH
SEE THE LARGEST LAND MAMMAL IN NORTH AMERICA

SEE THE GREAT PLAINS

GREAT PLAINS
ECOTOURISM
COALITION

CENTER FOR GREAT
PLAINS STUDIES,
LINCOLN, NEB.

VISITTHEPRAIRIE.COM

Find the posters at go.unl.edu/ecotourismposters

Find a 12-set postcard pack at
go.unl.edu/ecotourismpostcards

BISON REBIRTH
SEE THE LARGEST LAND MAMMAL IN NORTH AMERICA
SEE THE GREAT PLAINS
GREAT PLAINS ECOTOURISM COALITION
CENTER FOR GREAT PLAINS STUDIES, LINCOLN, NEB.

RAILS TO TRAILS
GIDDY UP DOWN THE COWBOY TRAIL
SEE THE GREAT PLAINS
GREAT PLAINS ECOTOURISM COALITION
CENTER FOR GREAT PLAINS STUDIES, LINCOLN, NEB.

BUTTERFLY BYWAY
BOOSTING BIODIVERSITY TO BENEFIT POLLINATORS
SEE THE GREAT PLAINS
GREAT PLAINS ECOTOURISM COALITION
CENTER FOR GREAT PLAINS STUDIES, LINCOLN, NEB.

CRANE COUNTRY
VISIT THE GREAT AMERICAN FLYWAY
SEE THE GREAT PLAINS
GREAT PLAINS ECOTOURISM COALITION
CENTER FOR GREAT PLAINS STUDIES, LINCOLN, NEB.

FLIGHTS OF FANCY
ON EVERY BIRDER'S BUCKET LIST
SEE THE GREAT PLAINS
GREAT PLAINS ECOTOURISM COALITION
CENTER FOR GREAT PLAINS STUDIES, LINCOLN, NEB.

FOSSIL FREEWAY
TAKE A TRIP BACK IN TIME
SEE THE GREAT PLAINS
GREAT PLAINS ECOTOURISM COALITION
CENTER FOR GREAT PLAINS STUDIES, LINCOLN, NEB.

PELICAN LAKE
A PRAIRIE PARADISE FOR WATER FOWL
SEE THE GREAT PLAINS
GREAT PLAINS ECOTOURISM COALITION
CENTER FOR GREAT PLAINS STUDIES, LINCOLN, NEB.

SEAS OF GRASS
CELEBRATE THE PULSE OF THE PLAINS
SEE THE GREAT PLAINS
GREAT PLAINS ECOTOURISM COALITION
CENTER FOR GREAT PLAINS STUDIES, LINCOLN, NEB.

DANCING CHICKENS
THE ORIGINAL SANDHILLS HOEDOWN
SEE THE GREAT PLAINS
GREAT PLAINS ECOTOURISM COALITION
CENTER FOR GREAT PLAINS STUDIES, LINCOLN, NEB.

PRAIRIE DOGS
SEE A TOWN UNDERGROUND
SEE THE GREAT PLAINS
GREAT PLAINS ECOTOURISM COALITION
CENTER FOR GREAT PLAINS STUDIES, LINCOLN, NEB.

SCENIC RIVERS
ENJOY PEACEFUL, MEANDERING WATERWAYS
SEE THE GREAT PLAINS
GREAT PLAINS ECOTOURISM COALITION
CENTER FOR GREAT PLAINS STUDIES, LINCOLN, NEB.

STARRY SKIES
SEE THE MILKY WAY LIKE NEVER BEFORE
SEE THE GREAT PLAINS
GREAT PLAINS ECOTOURISM COALITION
CENTER FOR GREAT PLAINS STUDIES, LINCOLN, NEB.

GREAT PLAINS ECOTOURISM COALITION

GREAT PLAINS ECOTOURISM COALITION · EST. 2014

CENTER FOR GREAT PLAINS STUDIES, LINCOLN, NEB.

VISITTHEPRAIRIE.COM